GREY GARDENS

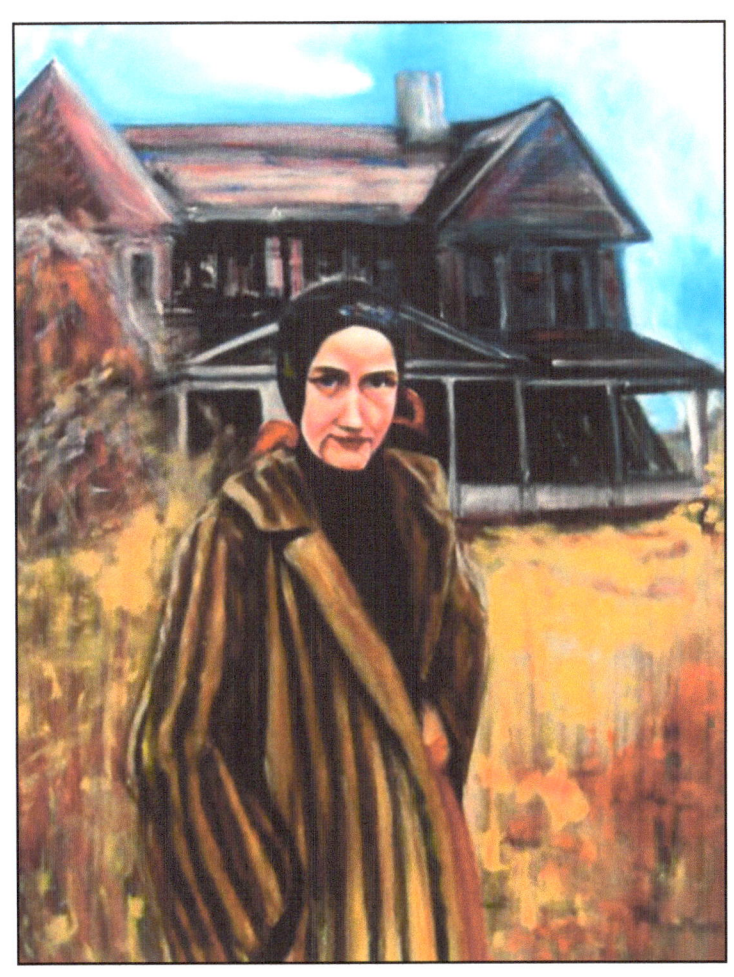

ART

GREY GARDENS ART

A SERIES OF PAINTINGS BY

ARTIST PACIFICO A. PALUMBO

ISBN 979-8-9885726-2-6

Printed in the United States of America

Booksmyth
Shelburne Falls, MA
www.booksmythpress.com

Contents

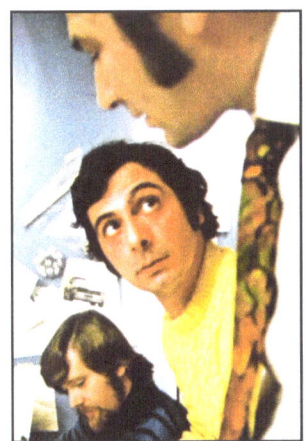
Pacifico Palumbo at Wells, Rich, Greene Advertising, NYC.

My acquaintance with Grey Gardens began in 1975 when I was working as an art director for Wells, Rich Greene, an advertising agency located in the General Motors Building on 59th Street and 5th Avenue in New York. Avery, a good friend who worked with me, asked if I wanted to join him to see a movie at lunch time. He said, "There is this movie called Grey Gardens playing at the Paris Theater on 58th Street. Do you want to go with me to see it? It is unusual and I think that you might like it."

And so began a venture that I have never forgotten. The movie was different all right, documenting the everyday lives of two reclusive, upper-class women, a mother and daughter both named Edith Beale, who lived in poverty at Grey Gardens, their derelict mansion in the wealthy Georgica Pond neighborhood of East Hampton, New York. Big Edie was Jackie Kennedy's aunt, and Little Edie was Jackie's first cousin. Watching the film I realized that one day I would paint some of the memorable scenes from the it.

Several years passed, then one day my partner saw an article about the movie in the *New York Times*. It spoke about the Maysles brothers and how they filmed it. There was a black and white photo of Little Edie looking in the mirror of her vanity. It had daffodils on it and it was covered with newspaper. She was wearing a fur coat. Big Edie, her mother, was sitting in the corner of the room. My partner said to me, "This is what you should be painting."

All of a sudden, I remembered how I was so impressed by the movie. I went online and found it on YouTube. I stopped at the frames that interested me the most and photographed them. I wound up creating thirteen paintings in all. I showed the paintings at the Latchis Theater in Brattleboro Vt., placing them in the lobby where people coming in to see the movies could view them. There were so many different reactions to them. I remember one person saying that the movie was a psychiatrist's delight, which made me laugh. Several years later I saw the play on Broadway.

Recently, as I was checking out Grey Gardens again on the internet, I came across "That Summer", a video about Grey Gardens created by Peter Beard. Two scenes interested me enough to paint them. One photo showed Little Edie sitting in a green chair that she had bought in 1965 at Bloomingdale's Department Store. The chair was left out in the garden for years. It was falling apart. Peter had Little Edie sit in it as he photographed her Another photo showed Little Edie talking with Peter who was holding a glass of wine in his hand. I painted both photos. I couldn't get over the people that visited Grey Gardens, such Andy Warhol, Truman Capote, Lee Radswell, plus many other important people.

So now I have fifteen paintings that I created based on the Grey Gardens photos. I created a website called GREY GARDENS ART on Facebook and I am currently looking for a gallery in East Hampton where Grey Gardens is located. I also saw the remake, by Hulu, of the movie featuring Drew Barrymore as Little Edie and Jessica Lange as Big Edie, which I recommend.

I hope you enjoy my paintings. They were certainly a delight for me to paint.

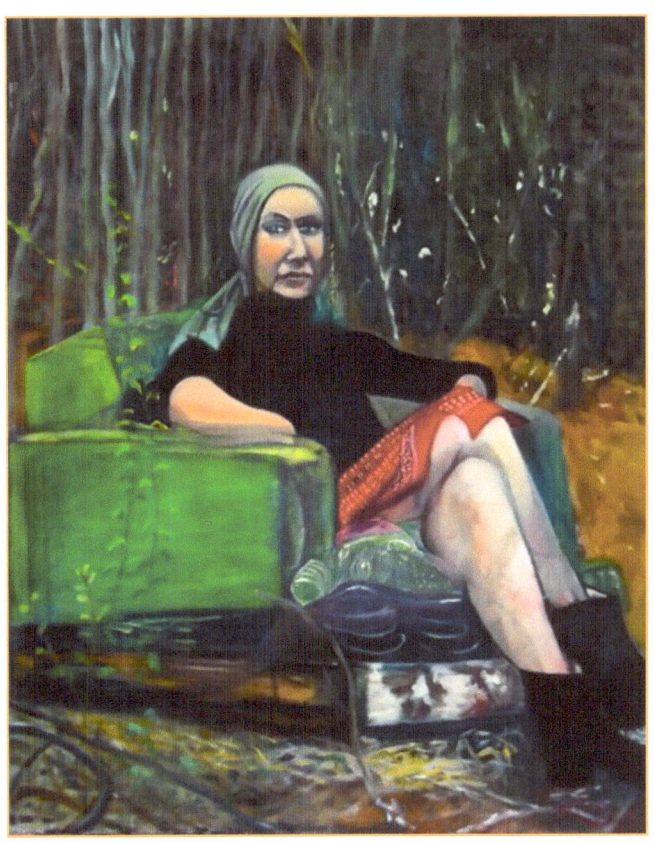

Little Edie in Bloomingdale's Chair

Paintings

12

GREY GARDENS

Big Edie in front garden

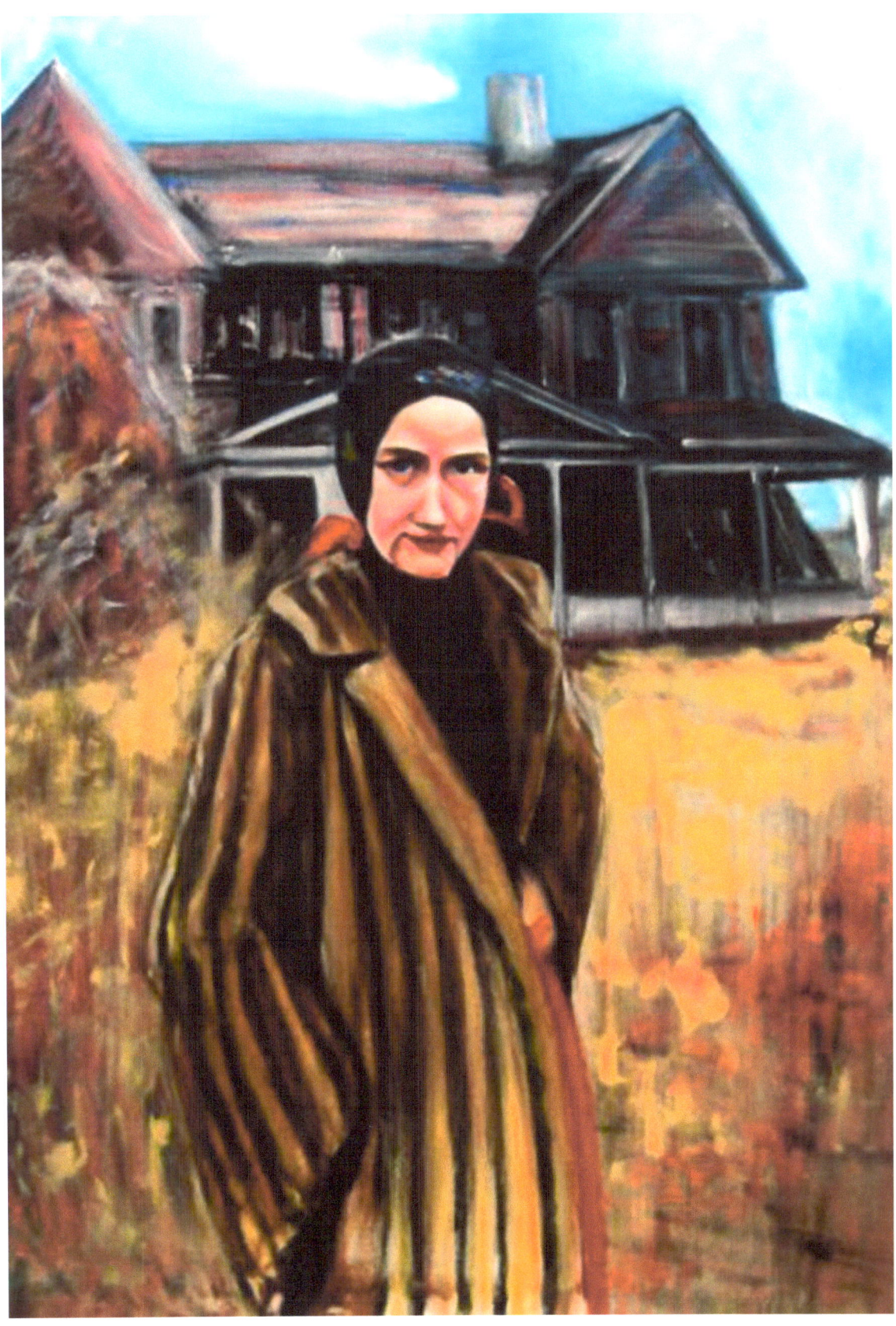

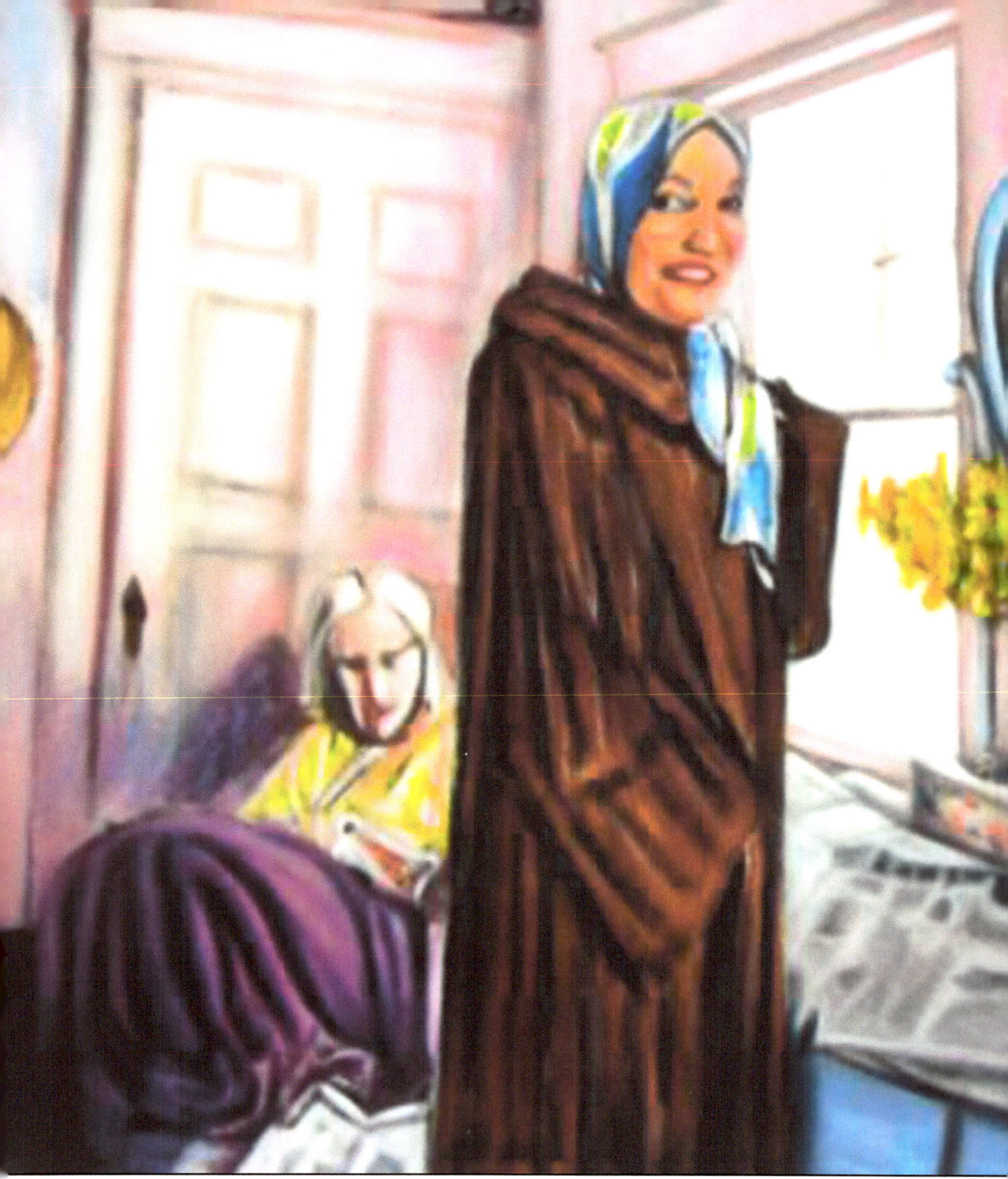

SPRING WILL COME

This is the first painting that I did in the series. It was inpsired by the black and white photgraph that I saw in the New York Times article about the movie

BIG EDIE IN BED

Big Edie and Little Edie slept in the same bedroom, but in seperate beds. This is where they would enjoy their cocktails in the evenings.

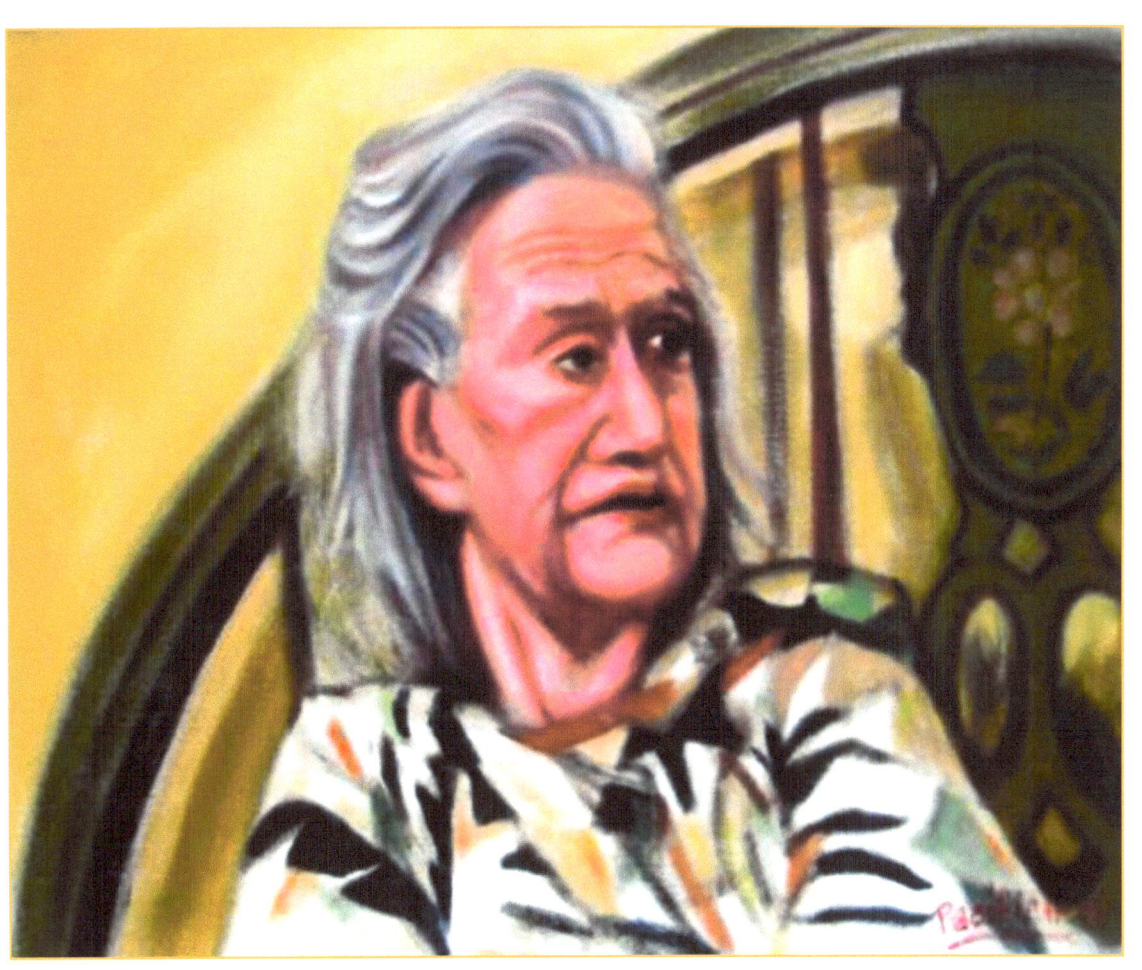

18

STAUNCHY

"I'm very staunchy" was Little Edie's favorite expression.

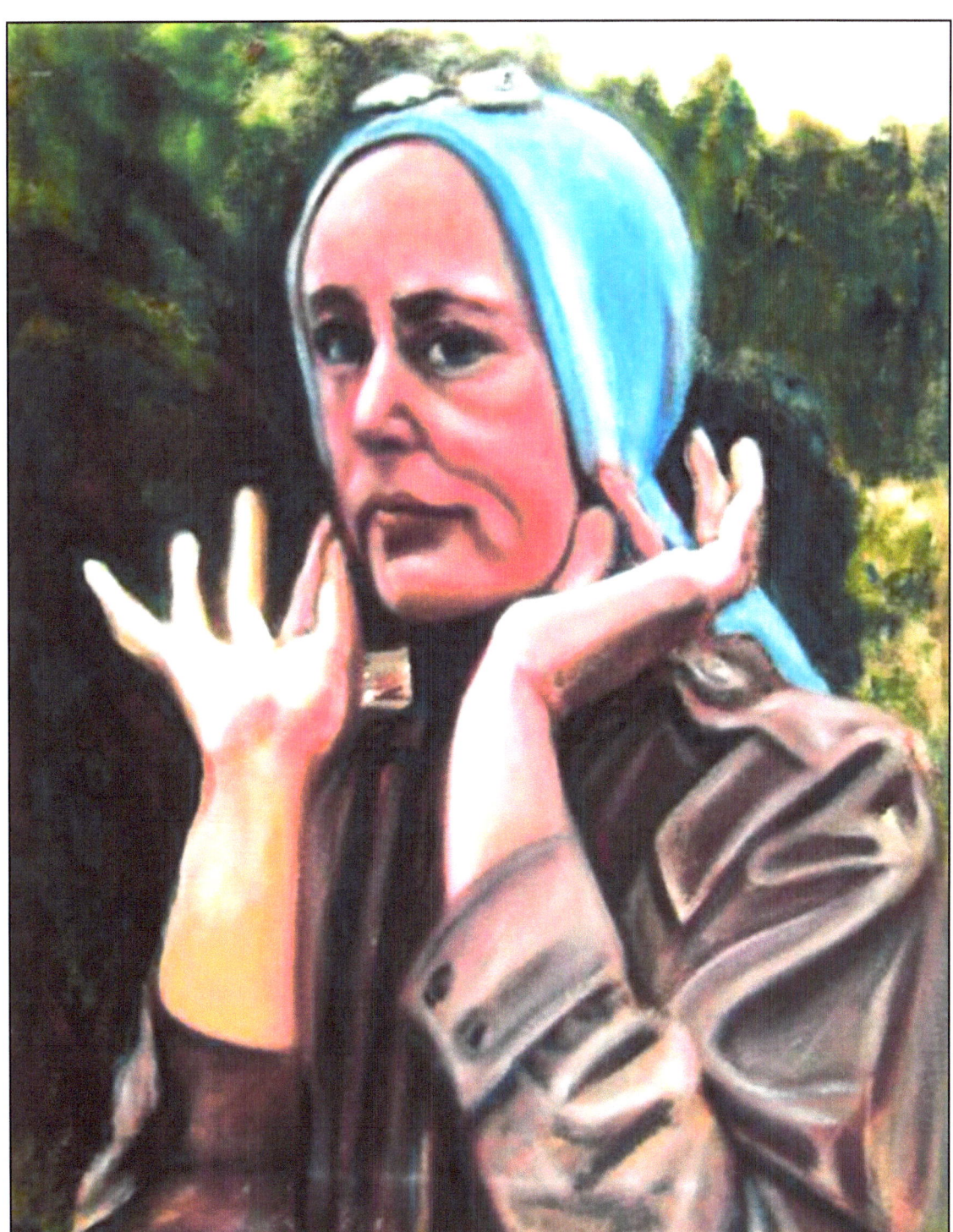

20

Tea for Two

This was Big Edie's favorite song, which she sang often.

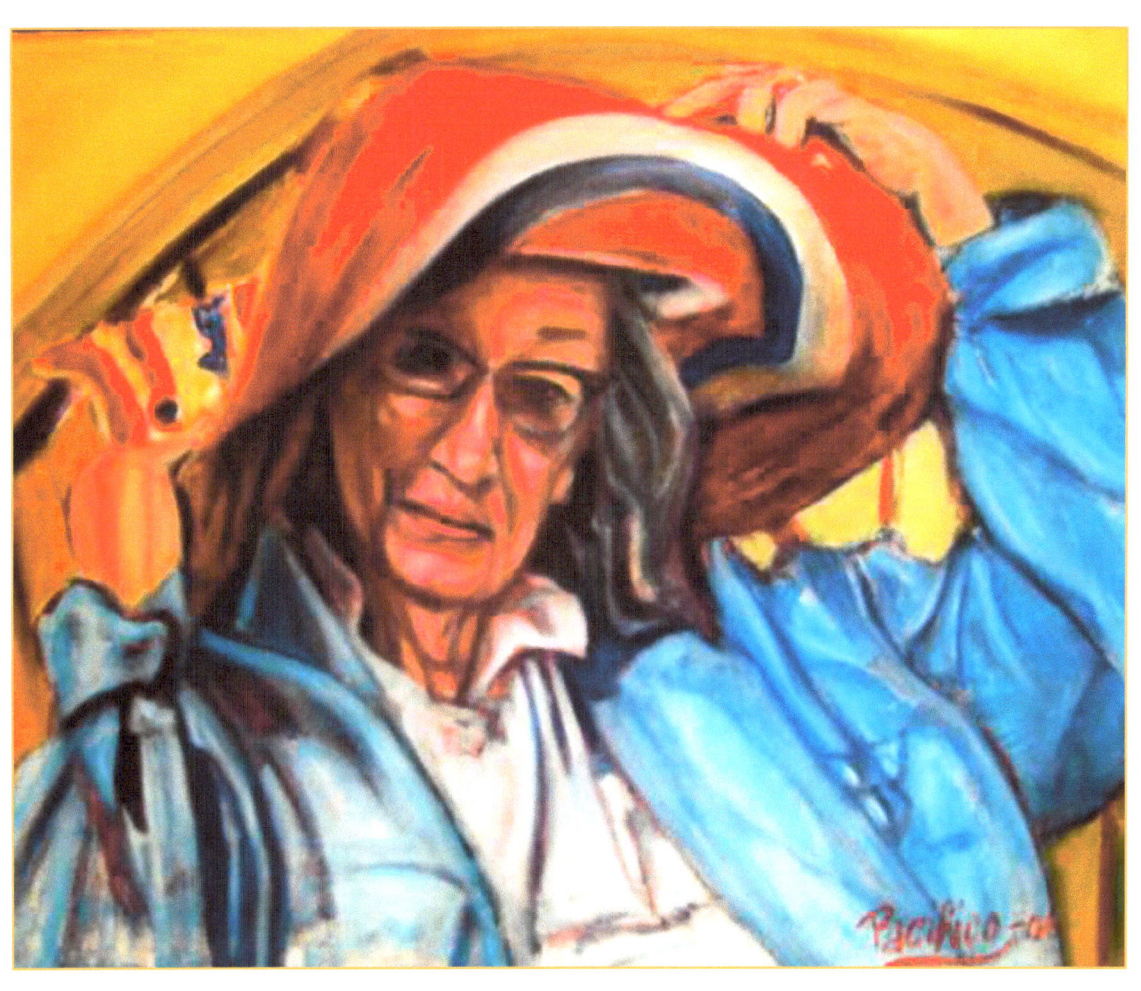

HAPPY BIRTHDAY

This is Little Edie's expression when listening to Happy Birthday being sung to her mother.

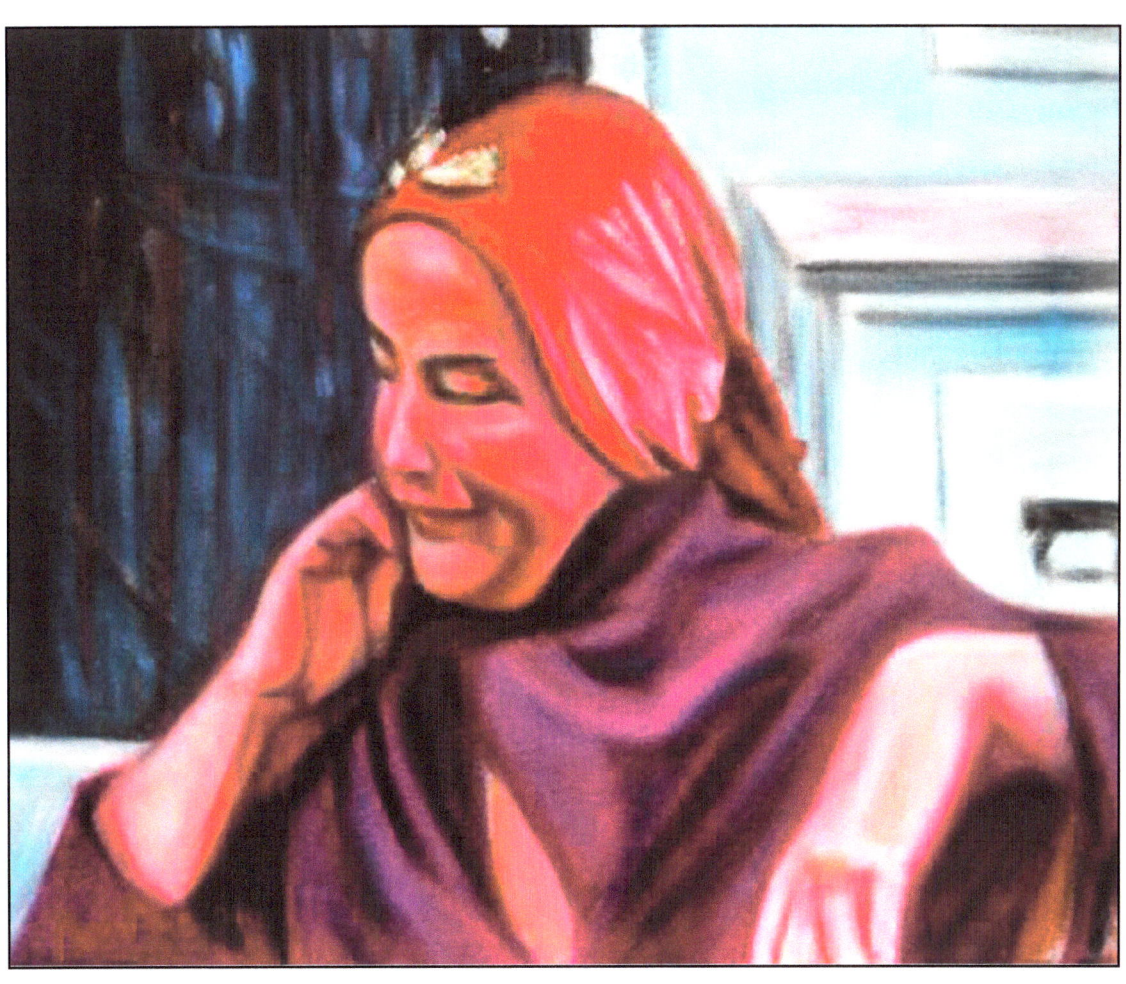

24

Libra Man

Little Edie was a Libra. She checked in a horoscope book to find out what a Libra Man would be like.

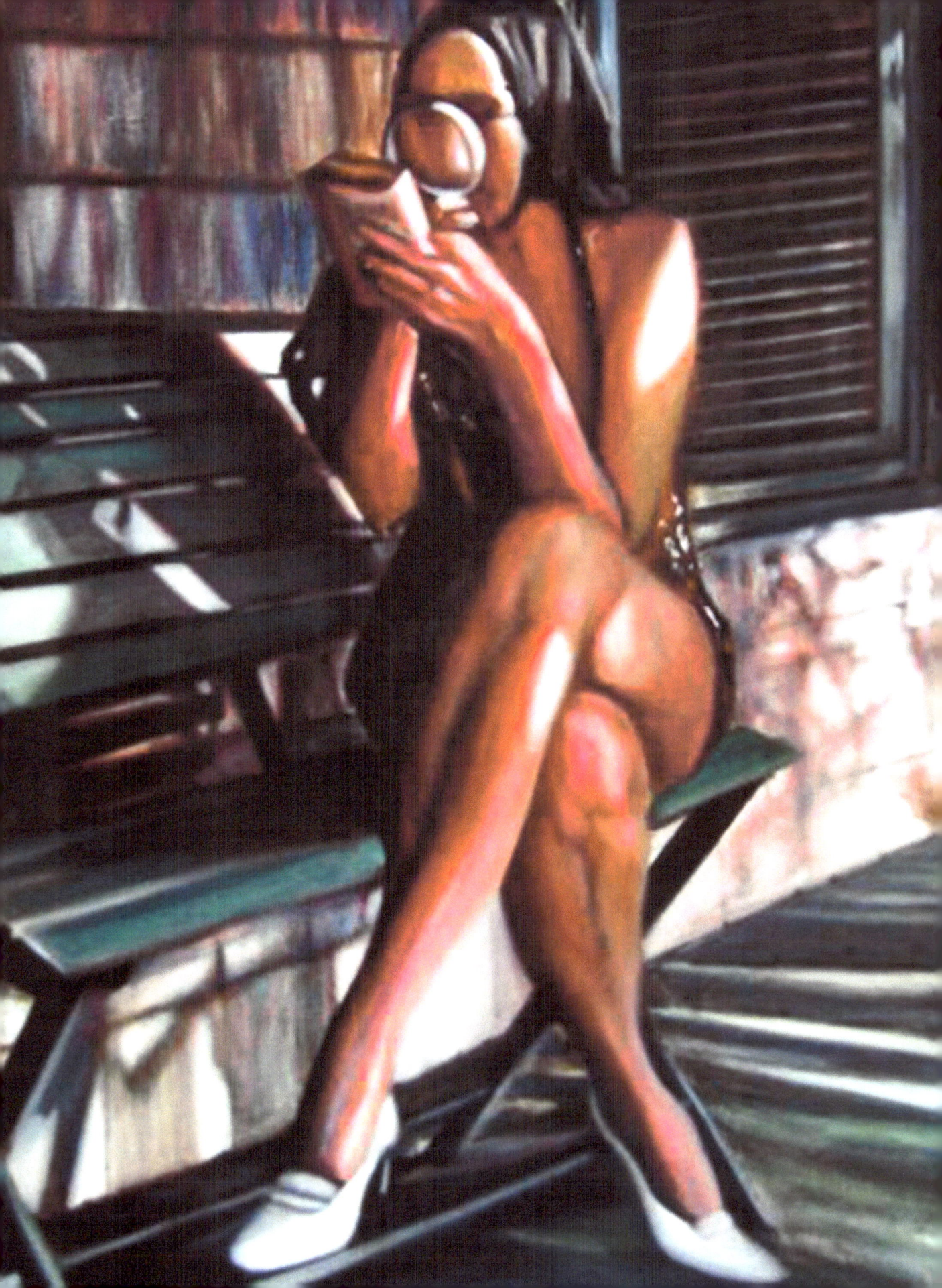

BEST OUTFIT OF THE DAY

Little Edie would create her outfits daily using what she found around the house including tablecoths and curtains.

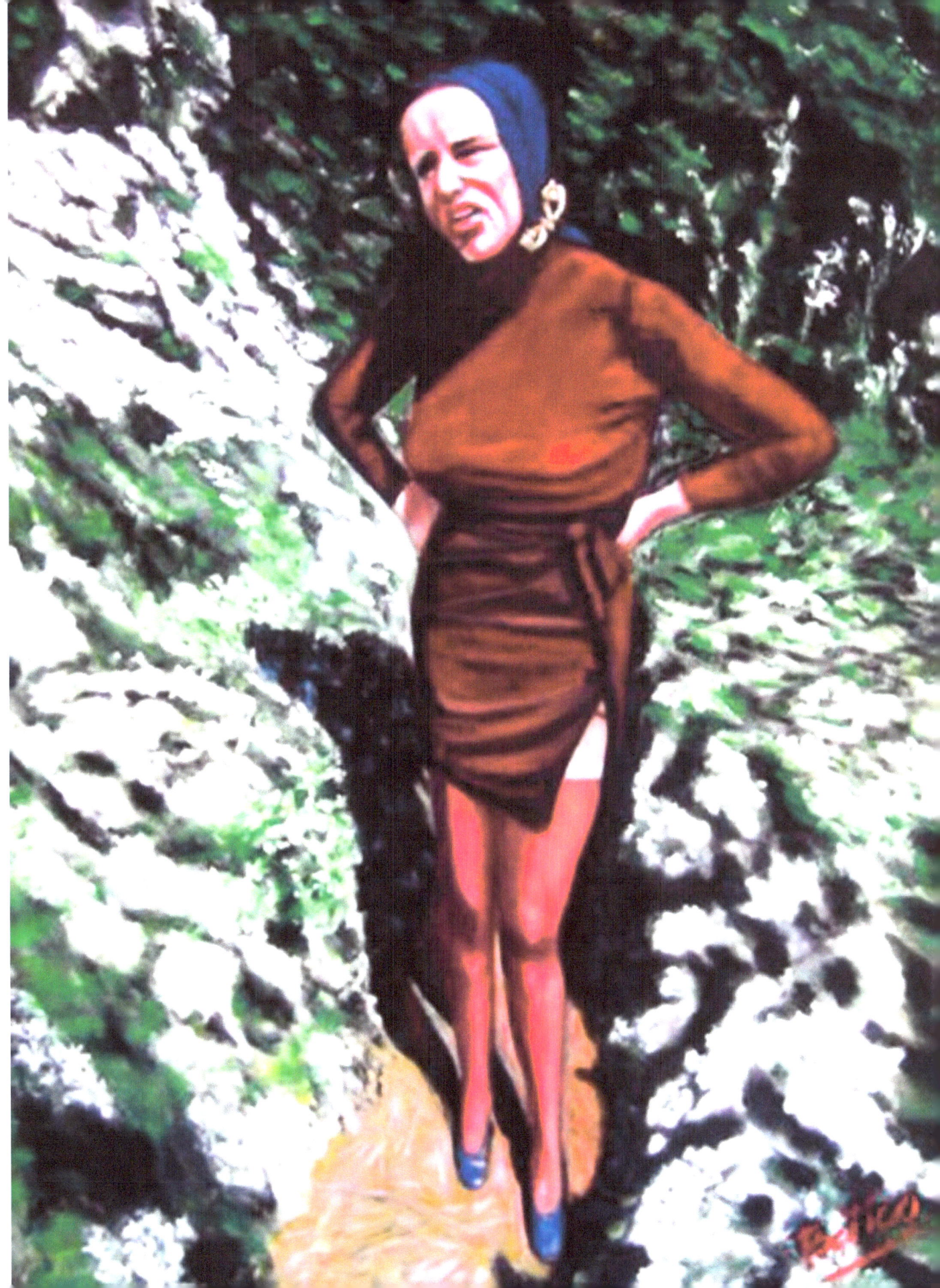

28

LITTLE EDIE IN BLOOMINGDALE'S CHAIR

From Peter Beard's "That Summer" video.

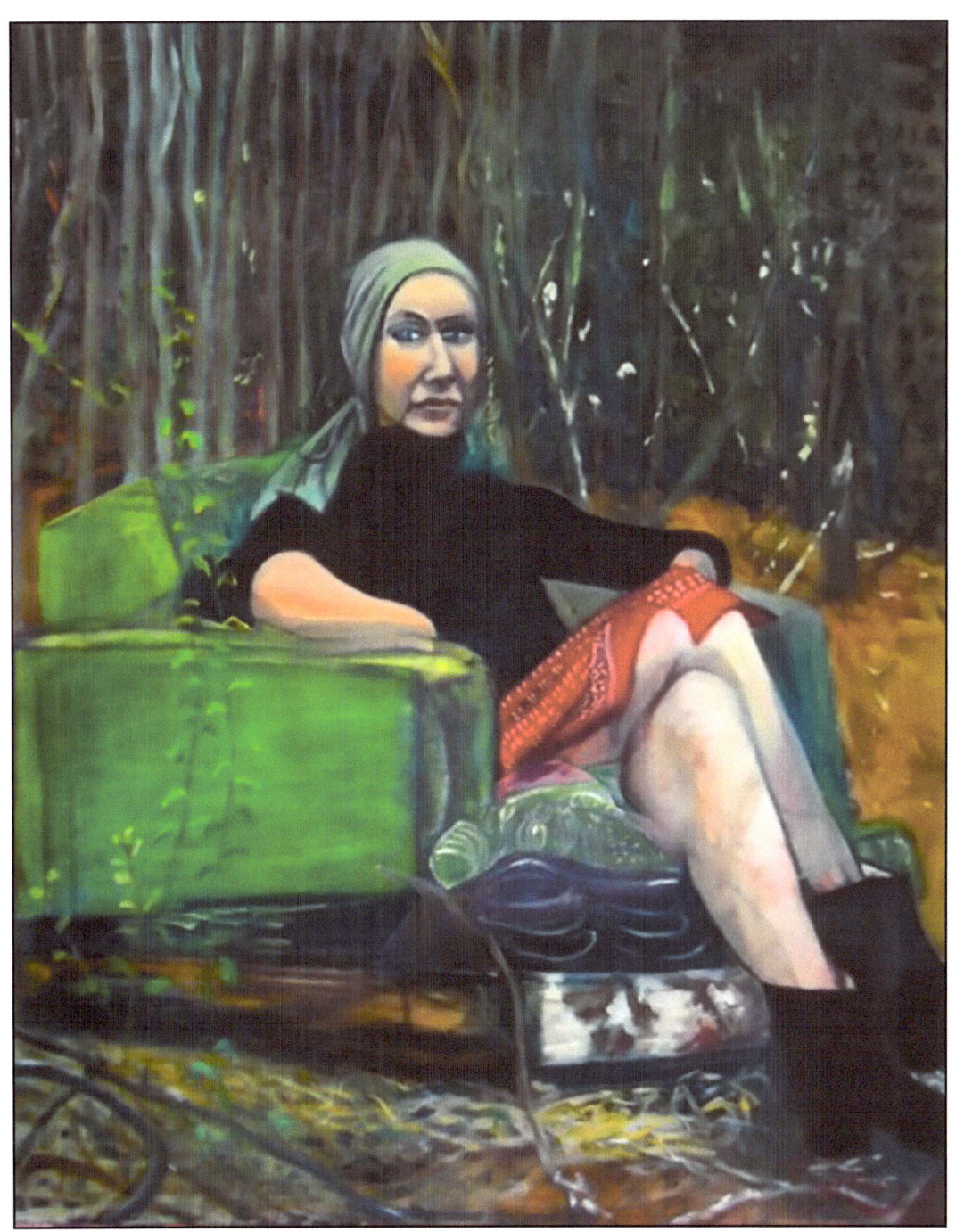

30

BED

Little Edie in bed.

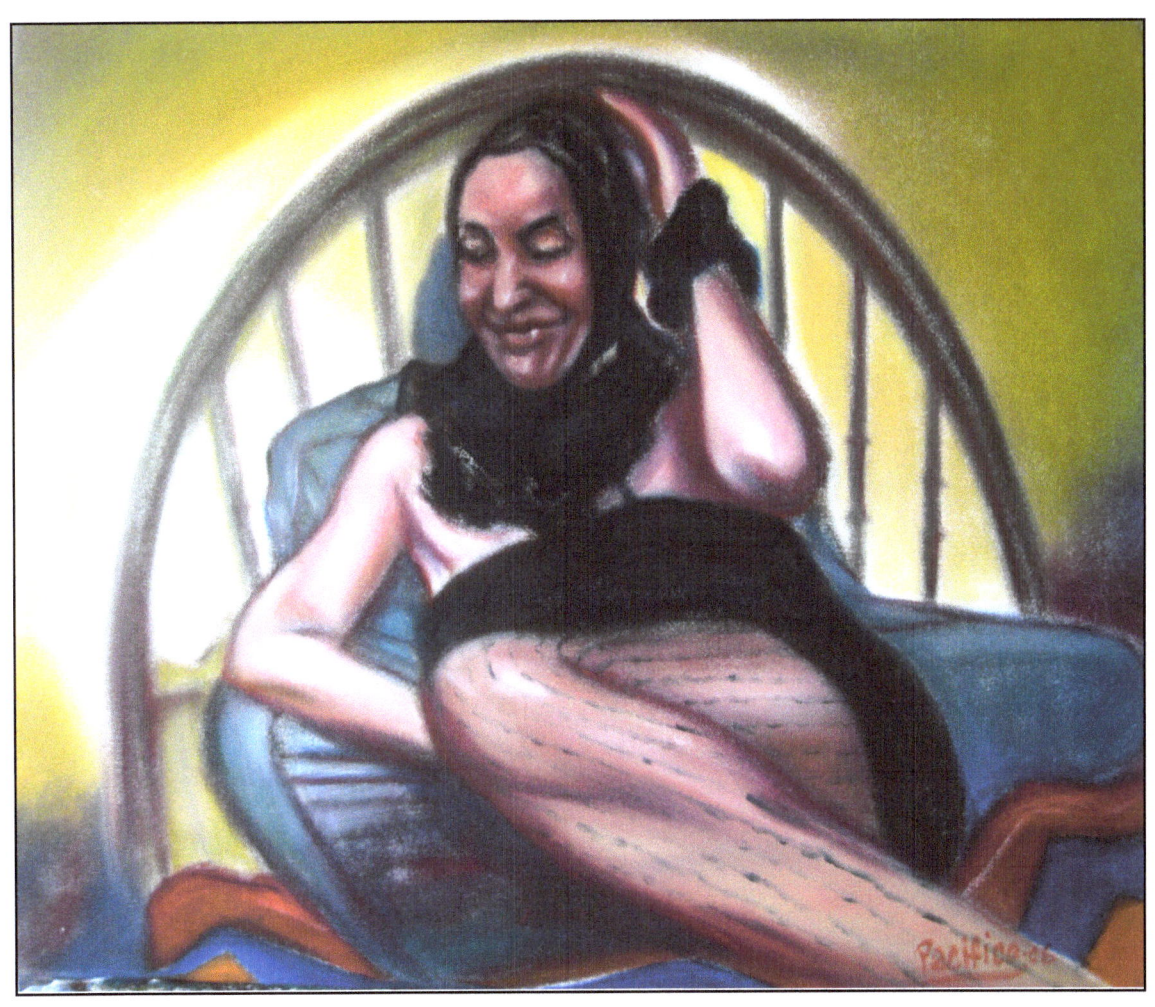

LITTLE EDIE AND PETER BEARD

From Peter Beard's "That Summer" video.

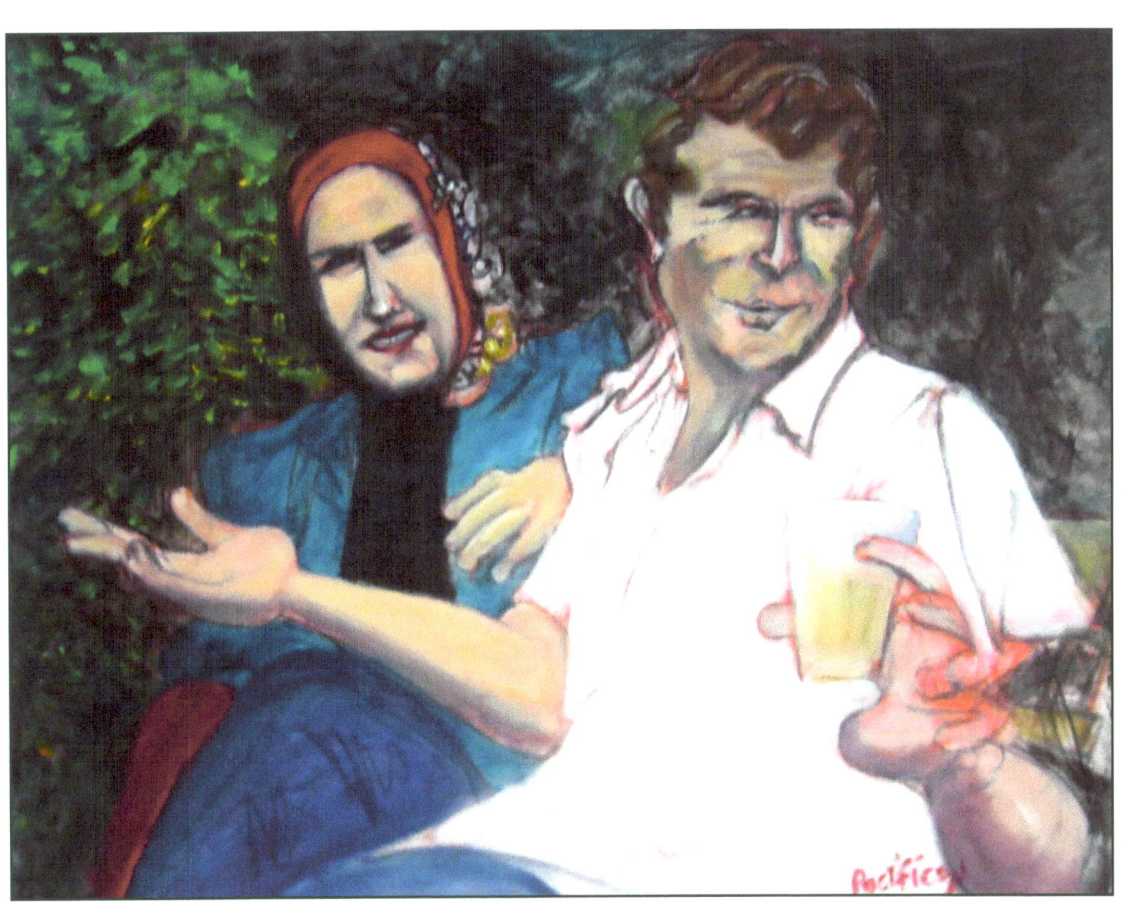

GETTING CORN

Little Edie went outside daily to see what groceries were delivered. They especially loved corn.

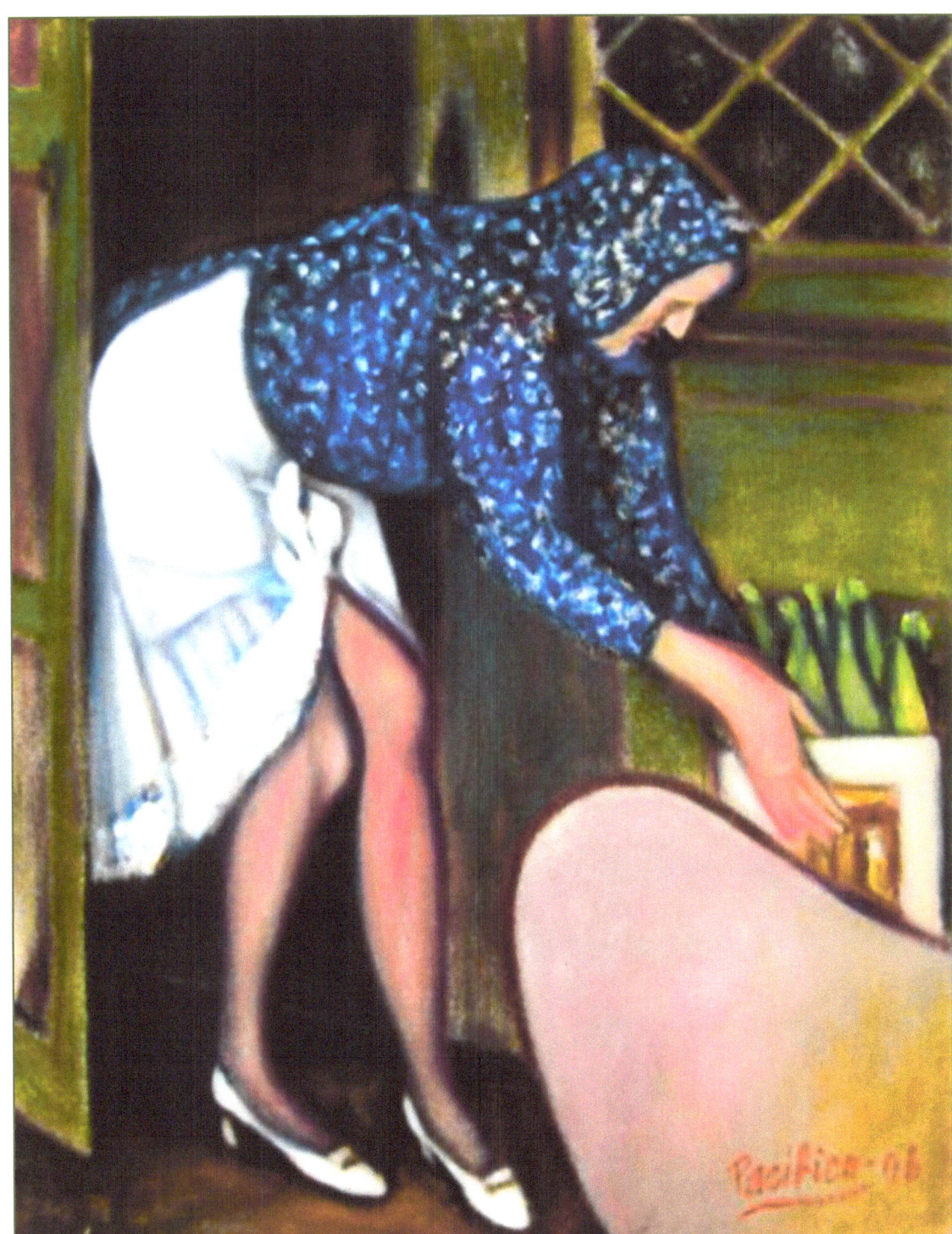

LITTLE EDIE DANCING IN THE HALLWAY

Little Edie practices her dancing regularly, ever hopeful of becoming a professional dancer.

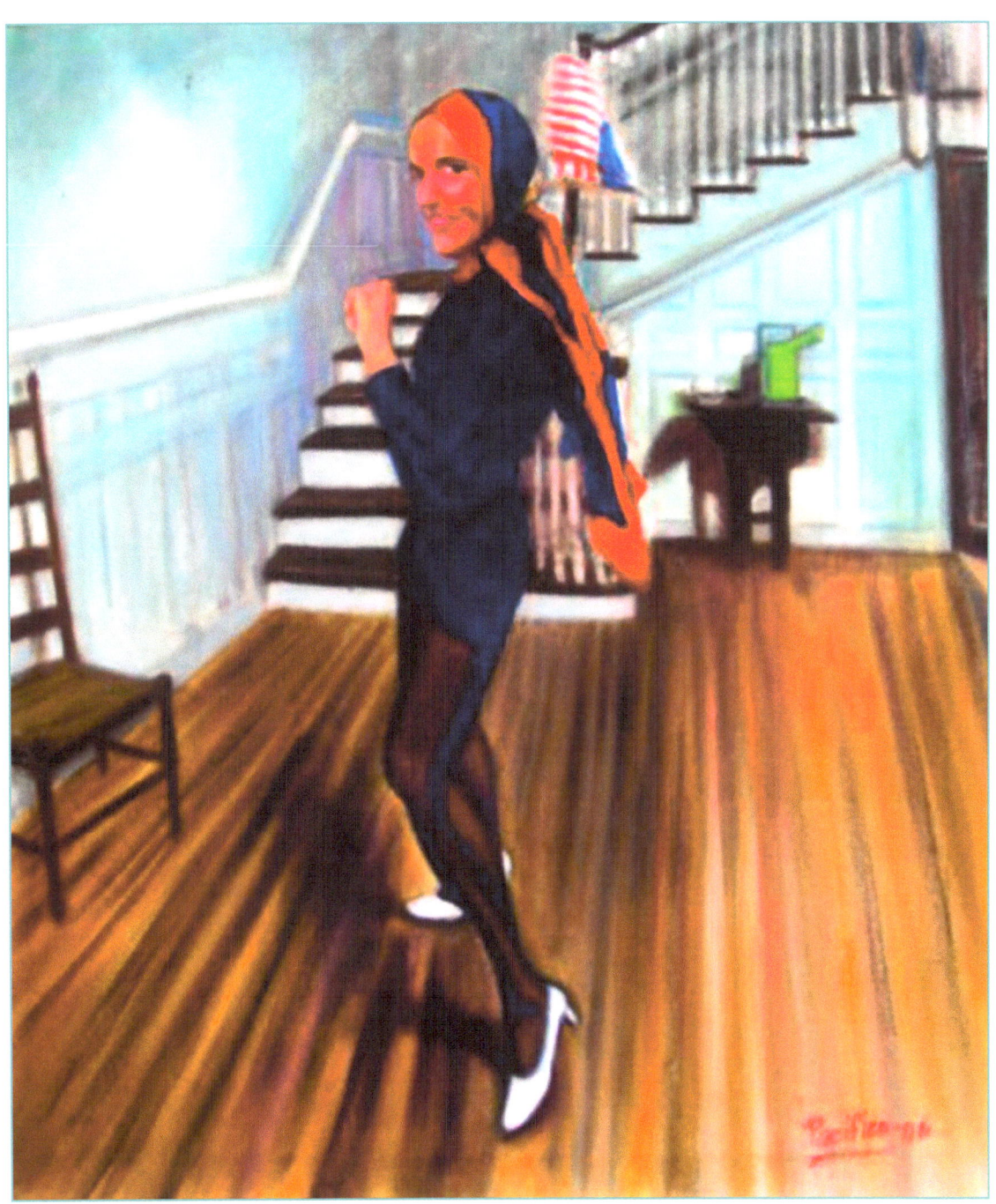

PORTRAIT OF YOUNG EDIE

Young Edie sitting in bed smiles as she is photographed.

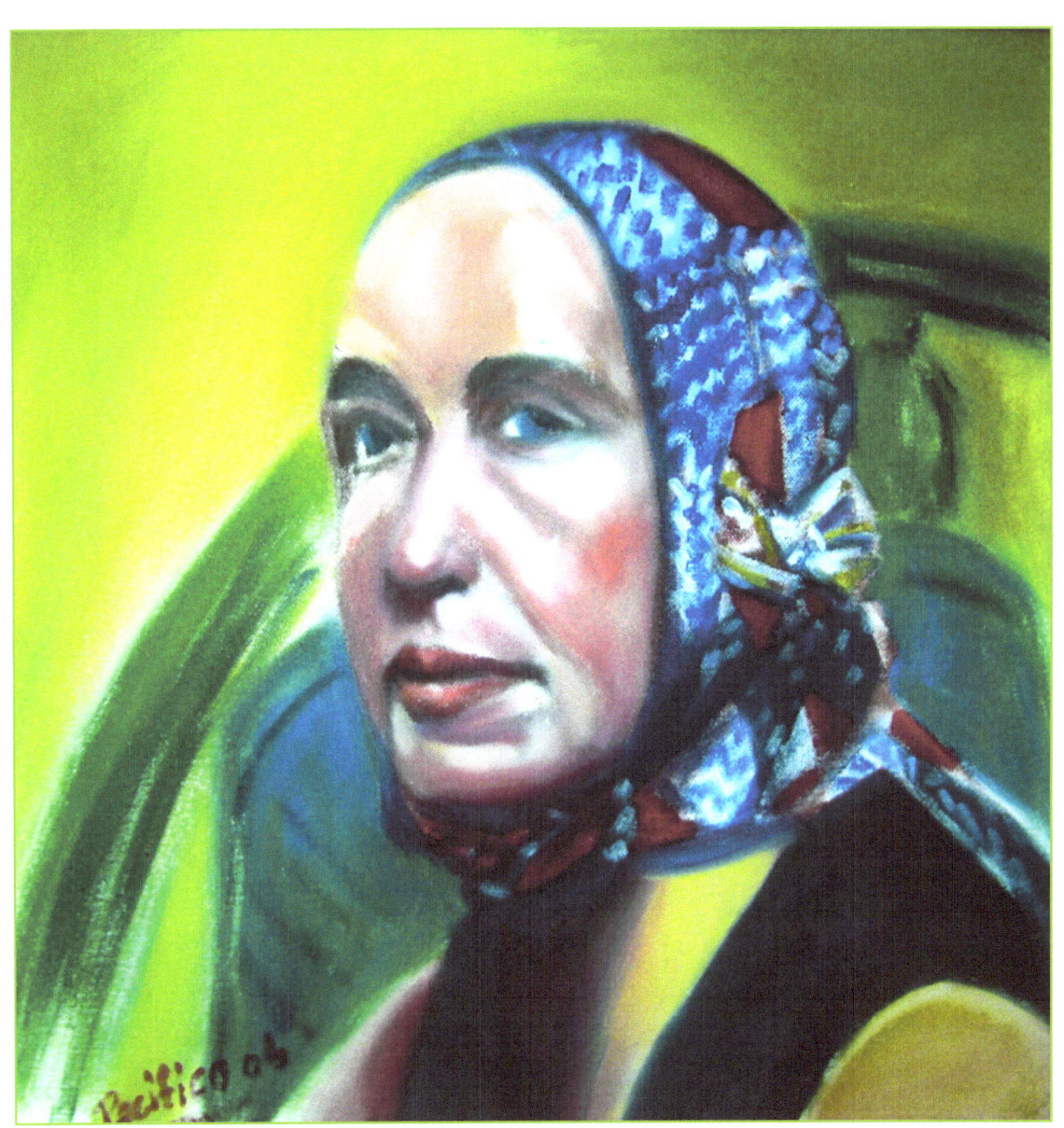

THROUGH THE BANISTER

Little Edie dances up a storm.

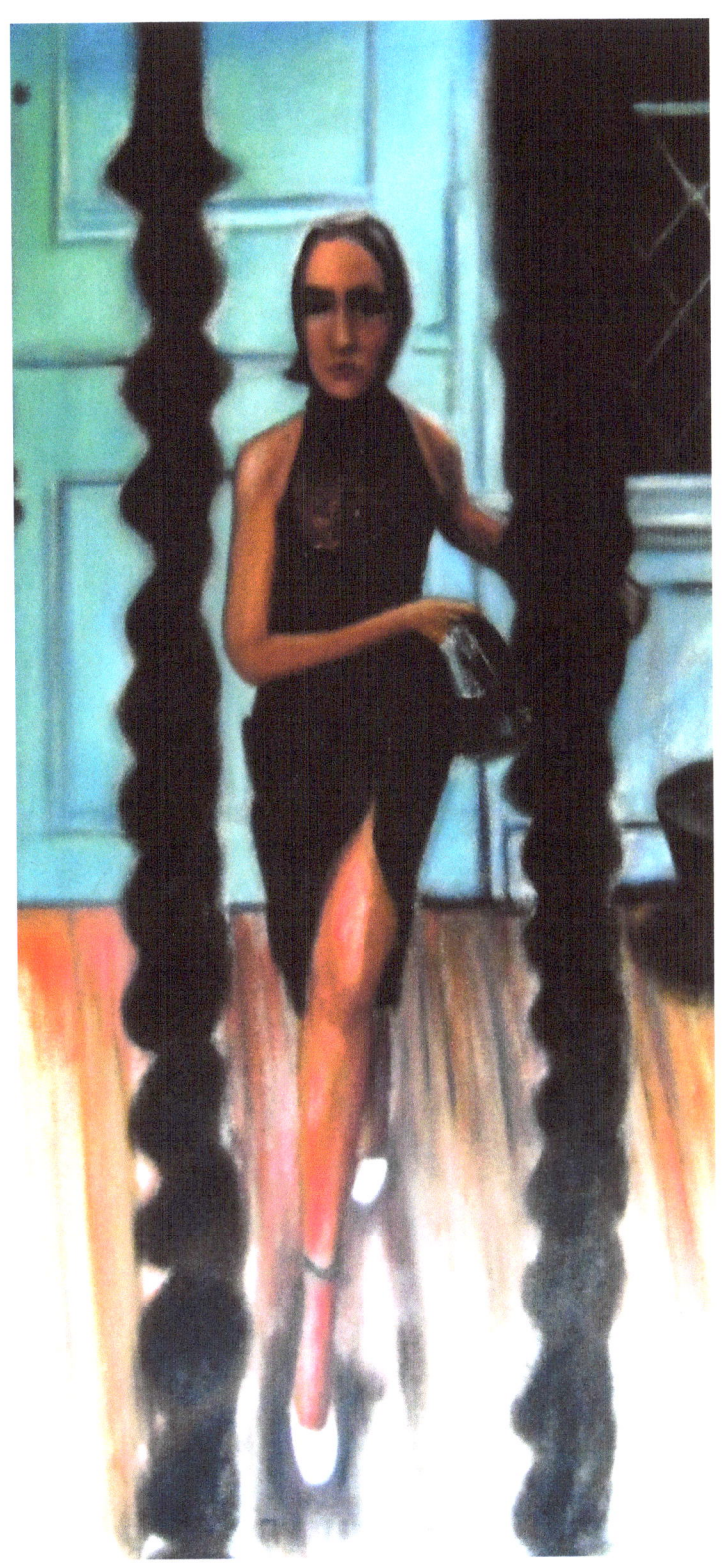